ISRAEL
AND THE
LAST DAYS

✡

Hal Lindsey

HARVEST HOUSE PUBLISHERS
Eugene, Oregon 97402

Except where otherwise indicated, all Scripture quotations are taken from the New American Standard Bible, Copyright © 1960, 1962, 1963, 1968, 1971, 1972, 1973, 1975, 1977 by The Lockman Foundation. Used by permission.

Verses marked NIV are taken from the Holy Bible, New International Version, Copyright © 1973, 1978, 1984 by the International Bible Society. Used by permission of Zondervan Bible Publishers.

ISRAEL AND THE LAST DAYS

Taken from **A Prophetical Walk Through the Holy Land**
Copyright © 1983 by Hal Lindsey
Published by Harvest House Publishers
Eugene, Oregon 97402

ISBN 0-89081-911-4

All rights reserved. No portion of this book may be reproduced in any form without the written permission of the Publisher.

Printed in the United States of America.

Contents

1

Israel, History's Greatest Wonder

◆

What other people has survived as a separate and distinct race for more than four thousand years in spite of a combination of the most formidable and destructive forces ever unleashed against any people in history? Neither four hundred years of slavery, nor two total destructions of their nation and land, nor two thousand years of dispersion in mostly hostile countries without a nation or homeland, nor unprecedented prejudice and persecution against the Hebrews has been able to destroy them as a distinct and separate race.

Every other conquered people has eventually merged and disappeared into the culture of its exile. Not so with Israel. She literally remained a nation in exile, though scattered into every nation on earth.

Miraculous Birth

Israel's origin as a race began as a miracle. A rich Mesopotamian named Abram from ancient

Ur of the Chaldees believed in the one true
Creator-God in the midst of rampant idolatry.
God called upon him to leave the comfort, wealth,
prestige, and security of his home and go as a
stranger to a dangerous and untamed land.

At a time when it was insanity to live outside
the security of a fortress city, God commanded
Abram to dwell in tents. This required great
faith on Abram's part and earned him a significant place in God's Hall of Fame recorded in
Hebrews, chapter eleven (Hebrews 11:8-19).

Because of Abram's faith in God's promise to
him concerning a son, God renamed him Abraham, which means "father of many nations."
After many trials of faith, the promised son,
whom God named Isaac ("laughter"), was born.
Isaac's birth was a miracle because both Abraham (one hundred years old) and Sarah (eighty-
six years old) were long past childbearing age.
From Isaac's birth onward, the history of Abraham's descendants through Isaac and his son
Jacob has been a pageant of triumphs and trage-
dies, ecstasies and agonies, punctuated by one
miracle after another. Through it all, whether
willingly or unwillingly, the sons of Abraham,
Isaac, and Jacob have been the vehicles through
whom God has revealed Himself to the world.

The greatest wonder of all concerning Israel
is that its history has been precisely foretold by
a number of Hebrew prophets. Every significant
event in the history of both the people and the
land of Israel has been predicted with 100-per-
cent accuracy. The following are but a few ex-
amples which we will look at in greater detail.

Promise: God revealed to Abraham that one of his descendants would be the source of blessing for all the nations (Genesis 12:1-4). The Messiah-Jesus' sacrificial death made forgiveness and salvation available to all nations (Isaiah 49:5-6, John 3:16-18).

Promise: It was foretold to Abraham that his descendants would be slaves for four hundred years in a land not their own (Genesis 15:13). The sons of Israel fled to Egypt to escape famine and remained there for four hundred years.

Promise: Abraham was told that his descendants would be delivered in the fourth generation and that the nation that enslaved them would be judged (Genesis 15:14-16). Through Moses and the great devastating judgments upon Egypt, God delivered the people of Israel (Exodus 1–15).

Promise: God told Abraham that He would lead the Israelites back to the land of Canaan and give it to them as an inheritance (Genesis 15:16-21). Under Moses, the people were brought back to the Promised Land. Under Joshua, they conquered most of it. According to many later prophecies, the greater fulfillment will come when the Messiah returns in the last days to deliver Israel.

A Sojourn in Egypt

Egypt has been an important factor in the history of God's dealings with His people Israel.

Throughout a good part of biblical history, Egypt was the cultural and intellectual center of the world.

Egypt had already been a great, advanced civilization for more than a thousand years when Abraham fled there for refuge because of a severe famine in Canaan. A few years after this visit, God gave Abraham a prophecy and promise concerning his descendants and Egypt: "And God said to Abram, 'Know for certain that your descendants will be strangers in a land that is not theirs, where they will be enslaved and oppressed four hundred years. But I will also judge the nation whom they will serve; and afterward they will come out with many possessions. And as for you, you shall go to your fathers in peace; you shall be buried at a good old age. Then in the fourth generation they shall return here, for the iniquity of the Amorites is not yet complete'" (Genesis 15:13-16).

This was a clear prophecy of the Israelites' long sojourn in Egypt. Abraham was given this prophecy long before his son Isaac was ever conceived, yet it was fulfilled to the letter in a most remarkable way. In the third generation—after Isaac was born, followed by Jacob and his sons—an unusual situation occurred. Joseph was the youngest of Jacob's sons, and he was loved by Jacob more than all the others. Jacob climaxed his favoritism toward Joseph by making him a multicolored tunic. The older brothers were jealous because of this partiality. The final straw that incited them to put their hatred into action was a dream that God gave Joseph forecasting Joseph's reign over them (Genesis 37:1-11).

The brothers seized Joseph and sold him as a slave to an Arab caravan, which in turn sold him as a slave to the Egyptians. Through God's providence, Joseph became a ruler in Egypt second only to Pharaoh. During famine in Canaan, Jacob and his family fled to Egypt and wound up under Joseph's rule and protection. When Joseph's identity eventually became known to his brothers, they were terrified and expected fearful reprisals after the death of their father Jacob. Joseph made a great statement of the divine viewpoint of life when he said, "Do not be afraid, for am I in God's place? And as for you, you meant evil against me, but God meant it for good in order to bring this present result, to preserve many people alive" (Genesis 50:19,20).

Abraham's Prophecy Fulfilled

Abraham's prophecy that "they would sojourn in a land not their own for four hundred years" began to be fulfilled with this providential move to Egypt. Joseph made a prophecy and promise to the children of Israel on his deathbed. He said, " 'I am about to die, but God will surely take care of you, and bring you up from this land to the land which He promised on oath to Abraham, to Isaac and to Jacob.' Then Joseph made the sons of Israel swear, saying 'God will surely visit you, and you shall carry my bones up from here' " (Genesis 50:24,25).

For the next approximately three hundred fifty years, the primary reminder to the Israelites of God's promised deliverance was Joseph's unburied coffin.

As the time of the final fulfillment of Abraham's prophecy drew near, Moses was born. Through divinely arranged, extraordinary circumstances, he became the adopted son of Pharaoh's daughter. He grew up in the court of Pharaoh and was the heir-apparent to his throne.

Moses had the best education Egypt could offer, and he was a genius in the fields of mathematics, physics, engineering, and architecture. According to ancient reports, he built one of the Pharaoh's crown cities. He was also a military genius, having commanded the Egyptian army in its defeat of the powerful Ethiopians. The Scriptures summarize this by saying, "Moses was educated in all the learning of the Egyptians, and he was a man of power in words and deeds" (Acts 7:22).

Moses' faith, when held up against the circumstances of his time, was awesome. There he was, a genius in many fields, the darling of Pharaoh and the Egyptian people, the heir-apparent to the throne of the most advanced, cultured, wealthy, and powerful nation on earth. Yet the Bible says, "By faith Moses, when he had grown up, refused to be called the son of Pharaoh's daughter; choosing rather to endure ill treatment with the people of God, than to enjoy the passing pleasures of sin; considering the reproach of the Messiah greater riches than the treasures

of Egypt; for he was looking to the reward"
(Hebrews 11:24-26).

After Moses chose to follow God's will for his
life, he had to be taught the paramount lesson of
spiritual success—that God doesn't work on the
basis of human strength or genius, but rather on
the basis of divine power released by man's
simple faith in His promises. It took God forty
years to train Moses for the job of delivering
Israel after he fled from Egypt, during which
time he earned his B.D. (backside of the desert
degree). Moses learned the hard way to be God-
confident rather than self-confident.

At last the metal of the man was ready to be
poured out of God's crucible. God sent Moses
back to Egypt at the age of eighty, just in time
to deliver the Israelites in exact fulfillment of
the prophecy that He had given to Abraham.
Through Moses, God unleashed devastating supernatural judgments against Egypt. The tenth
judgment brought the mightiest nation of that
day to its knees. Even the hardhearted Pharaoh
had to allow God's people to leave.

The Exodus

God led the people of Egypt by a pillar of a
cloud by day and a pillar of fire by night. The
Lord told Moses to camp in a shallow depression
of earth between Pi-hahiroth and Baal-zephon
with the Red Sea on the east. This, in effect, put
the Israelites in a cul-de-sac. The Lord told
Moses why: "For Pharaoh will say of the sons of

Israel, ''They are wandering *aimlessly in the land;* the wilderness has *shut them in*'' (Exodus 14:3).

God hardened Pharaoh's heart and he mobilized the mightiest army of that day. With hundreds of the most advanced chariots, he overtook Israel encamped in the cul-de-sac and immediately concluded what God had intended. Thinking that the Israelites were trapped, he ordered the horsemen and chariots to charge into the only opening of the cul-de-sac. From the human viewpoint, the Israelites were doomed to be slaughtered; they were a disorganized, untrained, and unarmed mob.

Why had God deliberately led His people into an apparently hopeless trap? How did God expect them to react?

God led them into this situation because He wanted them to learn to believe His promises. Both Abraham and Joseph had predicted that God would deliver them from Egyptian bondage and then would give them the Promised Land of Canaan. Ninety percent of Abraham's prophecy was already fulfilled to the letter. The Israelites did go to live as strangers in a nation not their own; they were made slaves and oppressed for four hundred years; and God did judge the nation that oppressed them. So God expected them to believe that He would fulfill the final phase of the prophecy.

Even with his back to the sea, Moses reminded the panic-stricken Hebrews of God's promise of deliverance. Time and time again they had seen

God prove His power and faithfulness as He brought supernatural judgments upon Egypt. Without the Hebrews' help, He had brought a mighty empire to its knees.

Now God expected the Israelites to look at the Egyptian army and the apparently absolute hopeless situation in the light of His promise. They had all the evidence they needed to justify such a step of faith. The Israelites should have prayed something like this: "Lord, we don't know how You are going to deal with this mighty army, but since You promised to take us to Canaan and give it to us, and since You have worked mighty miracles to bring us this far, we can't wait to see what You are going to do with the Egyptians!"

We have a similar situation today. The Lord Jesus has already done the greatest thing possible for us who believe in Him. He has pardoned all our sins by dying for them in our place. He has delivered us from death and given us new life empowered by the Holy Spirit. He has removed every barrier that stood between God and us. So when He allows trials to come into our lives, He wants us to realize that *He* allowed them in order to bless us and to teach us how to believe His promises.

Only one Israelite believed God that day—Moses. His faith in God's promises caused the Lord to open the Red Sea for His people and destroy the Egyptian army that tried to follow them.

2

Prophecies and Promises in the New Land

━━━━━ ◆ ━━━━━

After Moses died, Joshua took command of the Israelites. By the laying on of Moses' hands, he was commissioned and empowered by the Lord for the task of conquering the Promised Land. God gave Joshua several tremendous promises to claim in fulfilling his responsibility. I've meditated upon these promises many times and claimed them whenever God sent me out to do a difficult task. (See Joshua 1:3-9.)

General Joshua's battle plan for taking the land started with Jericho. This was a great fortress city which, according to modern archaeological research, was already several thousand years old in Joshua's day.

A great lesson of faith shines out of the conquest of Jericho. The Book of Numbers, chapters 13 and 14, records why the first generation of Israelites delivered from Egypt failed to enter the land of Canaan. They were afraid of its fortresses and especially the race of warrior giants called the Anakim. The following statement from the thirteenth chapter is a classic example of unbelief: "The land through which we have gone, in spying it out, is a land that devours its inhabitants; and all the people whom we saw in it are men of great size. There also we saw the nephilim [the sons of Anak were part of the Nephilim]; and we became like grasshoppers *in our own sight, and so we were in their sight*" (Numbers 13:32,33).

When a believer fails to look at a trial in the light of God's promised ability to cope with it, he simply becomes paralyzed with unbelief and fear. The Israelites saw themselves as grasshoppers, so naturally they thought the Canaanites saw them that way too.

But here is the lesson. Forty-five years later, Rahab of Jericho revealed what was really going on in the minds of the Canaanites when the Israelites first spied out the land and made their report to Moses. She told two Israelite spies, "I know that the Lord has given you the land, and the terror of you has fallen on us and that *all the inhabitants of the land have melted away before you. For we have heard how the Lord dried up the water of the Red Sea before you when you came out of Egypt*, and what you did to the two kings of the Amorites who were beyond the Jordan.... And when we heard it, our hearts melted and no courage remained in any man any longer because of you; for the Lord your God, He is God in heaven above and on earth beneath" (Joshua 2:9-11).

The Scriptures reveal that God had already prepared the way for quick victory. The report of the Egyptian army's incredible destruction at the Red Sea had apparently spread throughout the civilized world during the year that the Lord led Israel to Canaan. Egypt was the mightiest power of that day, so such an incident would have been awesome international news.

The record of Israel's failure to believe God's promises and the awful consequence—wandering in the Sinai wilderness for forty years—serves as a warning to us today. But what a wonderful challenge and hope the incident can give us as well! God wants us to immediately commit all trials to Him and to believe His promises that apply to the situation.

The Babylonian Captivity

Just before the Hebrews conquered the Promised Land, Moses predicted that Israel would twice be destroyed as a nation and twice be driven out of the land because of persistent unbelief. He also predicted that the first destruction and dispersion would come by the hand of one mighty nation. He specifically predicted that in this dispersion the Israelites would be taken captive into this *one* invading nation (Deuteronomy 28:49-57). This prophecy was fulfilled when the Babylonians destroyed Jerusalem in 586 B.C. and took the survivors back to Babylon as slaves (2 Chronicles 36:9-21).

Jeremiah predicted that the Israelites (who in Babylon were first called *Jews*, meaning "from

Judah") would be held captive for seventy years and then would be free to return to Israel (Jeremiah 29:10-11).

Isaiah added another detail to this same prophetic event. Two hundred years before it happened, he predicted that a Persian king named Cyrus would be God's instrument to set the Jews free and enable them to rebuild Jerusalem (Isaiah 44:28–45:6). Now, just think of how incredible this prophecy is! It foresaw the conquering of Israel by Babylon; the conquering of mighty Babylon by Medo-Persia and the ascendancy of Persia over the Medes, which at first was the more powerful of the two nations. Most amazing of all, it predicted the name of the first Persian king two hundred years before he was born as well as the return of the first wave of Jewish exiles and the reconstruction of Jerusalem.

The priests recorded the exact fulfillment of both Jeremiah and Isaiah's prophecy: "Now in the first year of Cyrus king of Persia—in order to fulfill the word of the Lord by the mouth of Jeremiah—the Lord stirred up the spirit of Cyrus king of Persia, so that he sent a proclamation throughout his kingdom, and also put it in writing, saying, 'Thus says Cyrus king of Persia, The Lord, The God of heaven, has given me all the kingdoms of the earth, and He has appointed me to build Him a house in Jerusalem, which is in Judah. Whosoever there is among you of all His people, may the Lord his God be with him, and let him go up'" (2 Chronicles 36:22,23).

Israel Scattered
Among the Nations

When Moses predicted the second destruction of the nation, he warned that the second dispersion would be much more extensive and severe than the first: "Then you will be left few in number, whereas you were as the stars of heaven for multitude, *because you did not obey the Lord your God*. And it will come about that as the Lord delighted over you to prosper you, and multiply you, so the Lord will delight over you to make you perish and destroy you; and you shall be torn from the land where you are entering to possess it. Moreover, the Lord will *scatter you among all peoples*, from one end of the earth to the other end of the earth.... And among those nations you shall find no rest, and there shall be no resting place for the sole of your foot; but there the Lord will give you a trembling heart, failing of eyes, and despair of soul. So your life shall hang in doubt before you; and you shall be in dread night and day; and shall have no assurance of your life" (Deuteronomy 28:62-66).

This part of Moses' prophecy was fulfilled in A.D. 70 when Titus and the Roman Tenth Legion crushed Jerusalem, destroyed the Temple and scattered the surviving Jews throughout the known world. So many were taken to the slave markets of Egypt that no one would buy them, fulfilling Moses' dread prediction of Deuteronomy 28:67.

Israel's Rebirth

Moses, Isaiah, Ezekiel, Amos, Zechariah and many other prophets predicted Israel's second restoration as a nation in the "latter days." They predicted that the Jews would return to their ancient homeland after a long and terrible dispersion among the nations, and that they would miraculously become a nation again (Ezekiel 36,37).

The most important factor in these prophecies is that God promises the Jews that once they have returned in the second restoration, their nation *will never be destroyed again*. However, the prophets do forecast that there will be a great war called "Armageddon" from which the Jews will be miraculously delivered. According to Ezekiel, this deliverance will bring great numbers of Israelites as well as Gentiles to faith in the true Messiah-Savior.

The dispute to trigger the war of Armageddon will arise between the Arabs and Israelis over the Temple Mount and Old Jerusalem (Zechariah 12:2-3), the most-contested and strategic piece of real estate in the world. Even now we are witnessing the escalation of that conflict.

3

Jerusalem's Place in the Prophetic Plan

━━━━━━ ◆ ━━━━━━

Jerusalem's importance in history is infinitely beyond its size and economic significance. From ages past, Jerusalem has been the most important city on this planet. Yet it never had the ingredients that have shaped and developed the world's major cities. It is not a seaport. It isn't on a great river. It was never on a main caravan or trade route.

Melchizedek came from this city to bless Abraham in 2000 B.C. (Jerusalem was then called Salem; see Genesis 14:17-24.) God directed Abraham to Jerusalem's Mount Moriah to offer his son Isaac as a sacrifice. When God spared Isaac by substituting a ram, Abraham called the place *Jehovah-Jireh*, which means "the place where the Lord will provide." God fulfilled that prophecy when He offered Jesus as a sacrifice for our sins on that very same mountain (Genesis 22:14).

David, the second king of Israel, conquered Jerusalem (then called *Jebus*) in about 996 B.C. He made it Israel's capital and placed the Ark of the Covenant there. From that time onward,

Jerusalem became the spiritual center of the world.

More prophecies have been made concerning Jerusalem than any other place on earth, and every prophecy has been exactly and literally fulfilled. Near the end of the eighth century B.C., Isaiah predicted that the mammoth army of the Assyrian king Sennacherib would not destroy or conquer Jerusalem although it seemed certain the city would fall. God defended Jerusalem against him and the prophecy was fulfilled (Isaiah 37:21-38). Isaiah also predicted that the Babylonians would destroy Jerusalem and sack its Temple—one hundred fifty years before the city was taken (Isaiah 39:1-8).

While in Babylonian exile, the prophet Daniel predicted an exact timetable for the major events affecting Jerusalem. He predicted the edict that commenced the reconstruction of the city and its Temple. He said that exactly four hundred eighty-three years after the signing of the edict, Messiah the Prince would appear in Jerusalem. He said that the Messiah would later be rejected and killed. Daniel then predicted the destruction of the city and the Temple.

The Temple

Artaxerxes Longimanus of Persia gave the edict to rebuild Jerusalem and the Temple in 444 B.C. Exactly four hundred eighty-three biblical (three hundred-sixty-day) years later, Jesus of Nazareth rode into Jerusalem on a donkey

(Zechariah 9:9) and for the first time allowed Himself to be proclaimed Messiah and the heir to David's throne (Luke 19:29-40).

Jesus entered the Temple area by the Golden Gate, or the Eastern Gate. The Eastern Gate ("Gate of the Place of Sunrise") was the main entrance to both Old and New Testament Jerusalem. The oldest and most famous gate of the city, it is the only one that led directly to the Temple. Jesus made His triumphal entry into Jerusalem through this gate, and He went through here on His way to pray in the Garden of Gethsemane.

The Eastern Gate was sealed by the Moslems centuries ago. Their reason for closing this famous gate is unclear, but in doing so they unwittingly fulfilled the first part of the prophecy in Ezekiel 44:1-6 (see 43:1-9): "Then He brought me back by the way of the outer gate of the sanctuary, which faces the east; and it was shut. And the Lord said to me, 'This gate shall be shut; it shall not be opened, and no one shall enter by it'" (Ezekiel 44:1,2). The rest of the prophecy will be fulfilled when the Prince, Messiah Jesus, once again enters the Temple Mount through this gate, this time to rule.

Jesus predicted the destruction of Jerusalem (Luke 19:41-44), saying it would occur in that generation (Matthew 23:34-39). Several days later, Jesus was crucified on Mount Moriah.

It was in A.D. 70, thirty-seven years after Jesus gave this prophecy, that Titus and his Roman legion destroyed Jerusalem and the Temple.

This was also an exact fulfillment of Daniel's prophecy (Daniel 9:24-26).

The final part of Daniel's prophetic timetable for Jerusalem and the Jewish people involves a seven-year period, commonly called the Tribulation. This will begin with the signing of a covenant between "the coming prince" of Rome and the leader of the Jewish people, called "the false prophet" (Daniel 9:27). This prophecy speaks of sacrifice and offerings which demand that the Jews rebuild the Temple for the third time upon its original site. At that point, Judaism and Islam will be placed on an inevitable course of war over the site, a war that will start Armageddon.

Many prophecies demand rebuilding of the ancient Temple, indicating that the event is a significant prophetic sign (see Matthew 24:15 and 2 Thessalonians 2:3,4). Therefore any move toward that direction is a crucial clue to what hour it is on God's prophetic timetable.

Today, devout religious Jews are increasingly desiring to build a new Temple on the Temple Mount. For years this seemed impossible, since most people assumed that the ancient Jewish Temple's foundation was somewhere under the Dome of the Rock, a Moslem holy place. But recent archaeological discoveries by Professor Asher Kaufman of Hebrew University have radically altered this conception.

The Temple Foundation Rediscovered

Dr. Kaufman, a professor of physics at Hebrew

University, has made the most exciting and important archaeological discovery of modern times. From the standpoint of biblical prophecy, it is one of the most crucial factors in a final alignment of predicted events that will precede the final seven years of history before the Messiah returns.

Dr. Kaufman, a crack archaeologist, spent sixteen years in intensive investigation on the Temple Mount before his findings were made known to the world in the March-April 1983 *Biblical Archaeology Review*.

Although all of the extensive evidence upon which Dr. Kaufman bases his establishment of the Temple foundation's exact location cannot be given here, a few of the most outstanding facts are highlighted in the following pages.

The First Clue

The most obvious clue that the Dome of the Rock *could not* be on the actual site of the ancient Jewish Temple is its position in relation to the important Eastern Gate. The golden-domed mosque is about one hundred meters south of a line drawn directly west from the Eastern Gate.

Ancient writings, including the *Mishnah*, indicate that the Eastern Gate led *directly* to the Temple, which faced eastward toward it. A line drawn from the center of the Eastern Gate, perpendicular to the city wall into which it was built, will pass right through the center of the Dome of the Tablets and the Spirits. This could not have been a mere coincidence; the Eastern Gate must have been purposely aligned with the place where the Ark of the Covenant rested within the holiest part of the Temple.

The Second Clue

The little cupola which now marks the place where the Ark of the Covenant stood and is known as the Dome of the Tablets and the Spirits has for centuries stood unnoticed at the northwest corner of the Temple platform, just inside of the arched entrance. (The cupola's location can be seen on the diagram on the next page.) Dr. Kaufman brings out the following amazing facts about this small dome.

First, it is situated over a smooth, flat rock mass that is actually part of the bedrock of Mount Moriah. It is only one meter lower than the only other exposed bedrock of the Temple area—the Temple Mount's highest point, over which the Dome of the Rock stands.

The bedrock under the cupola is unique in that it is flat and yet bears no evidence of having been shaped by tools. This site was obviously recognized as a holy place since no paving stones were ever placed over it, distinguishing it from the rest of the exposed Temple platform.

Second, the Moslems who originally built the Dome of the Rock complex in the eighth century gave this cupola two very important and revealing names. The first one is *Qubbat el-Arwah*, which means "the Dome of the Spirits." I believe

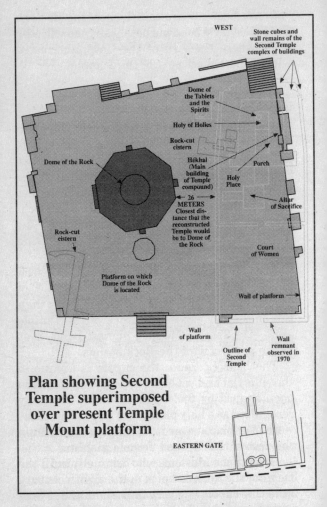

Plan showing Second Temple superimposed over present Temple Mount platform

WEST

Stone cubes and wall remains of the Second Temple complex of buildings

Dome of the Tablets and the Spirits

Holy of Holies

Rock-cut cistern

Hêkhal (Main building of Temple compound)

Porch

Dome of the Rock

Holy Place

Altar of Sacrifice

← 26 METERS Closest distance that the reconstructed Temple would be to Dome of the Rock

Rock-cut cistern

Court of Women

Platform on which Dome of the Rock is located

Wall of platform

Wall of platform

Outline of Second Temple

Wall remnant observed in 1970

EASTERN GATE

Diagram 1: Plan showing Second Temple superimposed over present Temple Mount platform.

with Dr. Kaufman that this was so named to preserve the memory of God's presence over the Mercy Seat, above the Ark of the Covenant, which sat on the flat bedrock unshaped by human hands.

The second Arabic name given to this cupola is *Qubbat el-Alouah*, which means "the Dome of the Tablets." I believe that this name was given to reverence the memory of the tablets of the Law given to Moses by the Lord on Mount Sinai and later placed inside the Ark of the Covenant.

Dr. Kaufman points out that both the *Tosefta* and the *Mishnah Yoma 5:2* say that the Ark of the Covenant rested on a "foundation stone" inside the Holy of Holies. I believe that this evidence, taken together with the exact measurements from many archaeological reference points that Dr. Kaufman has uncovered, established this bedrock as one of the holiest places on earth—the place where the manifest presence of God dwelt for centuries. This was a place so holy that only the high priest could enter it once a year with the blood of a divinely prescribed sacrifice (Leviticus 16).

The Third Clue

Dr. Kaufman traced the origin of the tradition that the large rock under the Dome of the Rock was part of the ancient Temple foundation back to a Moslem Jew of the eighth century, named Wahb ibn Monabbih. Both Moslems and Christians accepted and preserved this theory, and later it was even accepted by the Jews.

However, neither one of the two main theories about just what part of the Temple was built on top of the large rock inside the Dome of the Rock can be reconciled with the exact descriptions recorded in the *Mishnah*. (The *Mishnah* is a collection of laws, regulations, and customs which governed religious practice during the period of the Second Temple. This document is the richest source of information about the Second Temple.)

One theory places the site of the Temple's Holy of Holies on the large rock. According to Dr. Kaufman, this would be just about impossible. If the Temple foundation were laid out on the Mount from this reference point, the eastern wall of the Temple would practically be on top of the eastern wall of the city, in direct contradiction of the description presented in the *Mishnah*.

Another theory is that the large rock was the site of the altar of sacrifice. According to Dr. Kaufman, this too would be impossible. He says that the steep slope to the west of the large rock would have required the construction of a massive substructure in order to support the Temple building. However, there is absolutely no evidence of such a substructure from either literature or archaeological investigation.

The Fourth Clue

Once Dr. Kaufman found certain evidence on the Temple Mount, he could begin to predict the general location of specific stones and cisterns.

He did this through the detailed information concerning the Temple that is contained in the *Mishnah*, the *Tosefta*, and the writings of a Jewish historian named Josephus, who lived at the time of the Second Temple's destruction. (Diagram 1 identifies the various cisterns and foundation stones that were actually part of the Second Temple.) Through these lines of evidence, Dr. Kaufman had ample proof to establish the exact foundation of both the First and Second Jewish Temples.

I believe that Dr. Kaufman's dedicated and tireless investigation has provided the world with a priceless discovery.

I also believe that this discovery has accelerated the countdown to the events that will bring the Messiah Jesus back to earth. The reason for this belief is that the predicted Third Temple can now be built without disturbing the Dome of the Rock. As shown on the diagram, the Temple and its immediate guard wall could be rebuilt and still be twenty-six meters away from the Dome of the Rock.

Revelation chapter 11 indicates this very situation: "I was given a reed like a measuring rod and told, 'Go and measure the temple of God and the altar, and count the worshipers there. But exclude *the outer court*; do not measure it, because it has been given to the *Gentiles*. They will trample on the holy city for 42 months'" (Revelation 11:1,2 NIV).

The outer court, which includes the area where the Dome of the Rock is situated, was given to the Gentiles. So this prophecy accurately reflects the situation that is present today.

The stage is fully set for the False Prophet of Israel and the Antichrist of Rome to be revealed to the world and initiate the construction of the Third Temple.

It is mind-boggling to realize that this piece of bedrock, which was the site of the Ark of the Covenant and God's presence, will very soon be the place where the Antichrist will take his seat and proclaim himself God (2 Thessalonians 2:3,4). That act, according to the Lord Jesus (Matthew 24:15-22), will trigger the three-and-one-half-year-long Great Tribulation and the worst war of all time.

All of these things are tremendously exciting to those who know Bible prophecy. We are literally in the very last days of the Church Age. The Temple will be rebuilt soon!

4

Israel's Future Foretold

================ ◆ ================

Patmos is the Greek desert island where the Lord Jesus Christ revealed the final destiny of the world to the Apostle John, as recorded in the Book of Revelation, or the Apocalypse.

John tells us why he was sent here to die: "I, John, your brother and fellow partaker in the tribulation and kingdom and perseverance which are in Jesus, was on the island called Patmos, *because of the Word of God and the testimony of Jesus*" (Revelation 1:9). John was exiled to Patmos to starve to death because at the age of ninety he was still such a tiger that Rome couldn't shut him up. Roman judges kept telling him to stop proclaiming the gospel of Jesus Christ, but because of his faithfulness to God's Word he would not stop. So rather than make a public martyr of John, Rome sent him to die a slow, unknown death on Patmos. But God miraculously kept John alive and revealed to him a detailed prophecy of the destiny of mankind and planet Earth!

There are three keys to understanding this prophetic book. First, John constantly tells us that he actually *saw* and *heard* the incredible wars and global catastrophes, and that he was commanded to write about them. How could this first-century man describe the scientific wonders of the latter twentieth century? He had to illustrate them with phenomena of the first century; for instance, a thermonuclear war looked to him like a giant volcanic eruption spewing fire and brimstone.

Second, the outline of the book is given in Revelation 1:19. John was commanded to write about "the things that he had seen" (chapter 1), "the things which are" (chapters 2 and 3), and "the things which shall take place after these things" (chapters 4 through 22). Chapters 4 through 18 specifically detail the events of the seven-year Tribulation that immediately precedes the return of the Lord Messiah, Jesus. Chapter 19 predicts the Second Advent of Jesus, with accompanying phenomena.

Third, most figures of speech used by the Apostle John are either explained in the context or in some other book of the Bible. They can be quickly traced with the help of a good Bible concordance.

It is very important to remember the first key to the Book of Revelation, however. Much of the symbolism John used was the result of a first-century man being catapulted in God's time machine up to the end of the twentieth century, then returned to his own time and commanded to write about what he had seen and heard. The only way that John could obey that instruction was to use phenomena with which he was familiar to illustrate the scientific and technical marvels that he predicts.

As I contemplate the isolation and remoteness of the Isle of Patmos in John's day, how ironic it seems to me that from here the rise and fall of all civilization was predicted! And all of the events that John foresaw are coming together today in the precise pattern he predicted. To emphasize the nearness of the Lord's return, I want to point out a few of the specific prophetic signs that are being fulfilled simultaneously before our eyes:

- Israel has been reborn as a nation.

- Jerusalem is in Jewish hands.

- The Arab nations are united in a fanatical obsession to destroy Israel.

- The Soviet Union has fulfilled the prophecies of the great, murderous power to the extreme north of Israel.

- The Chinese are building the great army of two hundred million that will march across the dried-up Euphrates River (Revelation 16:12).

- The European Community is rising out of the old Roman culture (Daniel 7:24-25; Revelation 13 and 17).

- World conditions are ripe for the rise of the Antichrist.

Science Has Set
the Stage

Scientific and technical developments have reached the point where some key prophecies of the Book of Revelation can now be fulfilled. Thermonuclear weapons can do every horrible thing that John predicts in 6:12-17 and 8:7-12. In fact, I believe that he is describing a thermonuclear war when he says, "...and something like a great mountain burning with fire was thrown into the sea; and a third of the sea became blood; and a third of the creatures, which were in the sea and had life, died, and a third of the ships were destroyed" (Revelation 8:8-9).

When a hydrogen warhead explodes in the sea, it looks like a great mountain laced with fire. The Soviet Union has amassed the largest nuclear-missile-firing navy in history, and the West is racing to catch up. I believe that this generation will witness the greatest naval battle of all time—as part of the War of Armageddon predicted by John.

The super computers are another relevant technical development. John foresaw the Antichrist and his cohort, the False Prophet of Israel, force all the people of the world to receive a number. Without this number, no one could buy or sell or hold a job. The prefix of this number will be 666. When in history could any dictator number every person on earth? The technology did not exist before the advent of super computers. (See Revelation 13:16-18.)

The Final Battle

The vortex of the final battles of world history will be in the valley below Megiddo, which is prophetically called the Valley of Armageddon (Revelation 16:16).

Megiddo was a fortified city overlooking the fertile Jezreel Valley in northern Israel. It saw continuous warfare throughout most of its active history, which extended from 4000 B.C. to around 400 B.C. Extensive archaeological excavations have uncovered twenty cities built one upon another, as various wars left the city in ruins.

The reasons for this frequent warfare are easy to find. First, Megiddo sits upon a hill which commanded the main caravan route from Egypt and Africa to ancient Phoenicia, Assyria, Babylon, and later, Persia. Second, Megiddo is located in the middle of a natural "land bridge" that connects Africa, Asia, and Europe. This land bridge begins in the north at the Bosporus, a vital narrow waterway which passes through Istanbul to the Black Sea. It extends southward through what is now Turkey, Syria, Lebanon, Israel, and Sinai. In ancient times the southern end of the land bridge began with the border of Egypt. Today it begins with that crucial sea lane, the Suez Canal.

Almost all of the would-be conquerors of the past fought to possess Megiddo because of its strategic location. When the Apostle John wrote the Book of Revelation, Megiddo was a name already well-associated with turmoil because of its strategic position on the land bridge.

The central prophecy of the *Armageddon War* is found in Revelation 16:12-16. There are several important points to observe.

• Armageddon is not a single battle, but a campaign or an extended war. Armageddon is described as "the war [*polemos* in Greek] of the great day of God, the Almighty" (Revelation 16:14). *Polemos* means an extended campaign, not just one battle.

• Armageddon is inextricably connected with two great world movements of armies. First the awesome armies of "the Kings of the East," which will be led by China and number two hundred million, are mustered from east of the Euphrates. The Euphrates River, which is the ancient boundary between East and West, is then miraculously dried up by an angel of God. This facilitates the Chinese armies' invasion of the Middle East (Revelation 16:12). Second, Satan, the Roman Antichrist, and the Jewish False Prophet use demonic deception to gather the rest of the armies from "the whole world" to counter the invasion from the East.

The final war begins in the middle of the Tribulation when the "Abomination of Desolation" is set up in Jerusalem's Third Temple.

The following four maps illustrate the stages of the Armageddon campaign, from the mobilization of the world's armies against Israel to the miraculous conversion and deliverance of God's people.

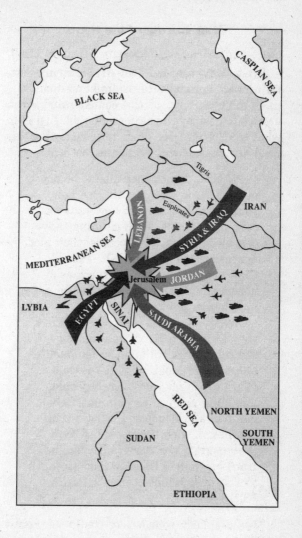

Map 1

Map 1: King of the South

Pan-Arabic Armies Attack Israel. (Daniel 11:40)

First, Egyptian-led Pan-Arabic armies attack Israel. Long ago the psalmist predicted the final mad attempt of the confederated Arab armies to destroy the nation of Israel. Listen to what the Spirit of God predicted concerning this final attack that will begin the last war:

> "O God, do not keep silent; be not quiet, O God, be not still. See how your enemies are astir, how your foes rear their heads. With cunning they conspire against your people; they plot against those you cherish. 'Come,' they say, 'Let us destroy them as a *nation*, that the name of *Israel* be remembered no more.'
>
> "With one mind they plot together; they form an *alliance* against *you*— the tents of Edom and the Ishmaelites [Jordan], of Moab and the descendants of Hagar [most Arab people, including modern Egyptians], Gebal, Ammon and Amalek, Philistia [Palestinians], with the people of Tyre [Lebanon]. Even Assyria [Syria and Iraq] has joined them to lend strength to the descendants of Lot" (Psalm 83:1-8 NIV).

This prophecy sounds like Radio Damascus when it says, "Come, let us destroy them as a nation, that the name of Israel be remembered no more"!

The psalmist's prophecy quoted above indicates which armies will launch the initial attack. The prophet Daniel briefly describes this dreadful invasion: "At the time of the end [the middle of the Tribulation] the king of the South [the Egyptian-led Pan-Arabic armies] will engage him [Israeli False Prophet] in battle..." (Daniel 11:40 NIV).

The conditions in the Middle East are already setting the stage for this attack. The whole world is concerned about the volatile Arab-Israeli conflict that is always close to igniting a global war.

• The Palestinians are determined to trouble the world until they repossess what they feel is their land.

• The Arab nations consider it a matter of racial honor to destroy the State of Israel.

• Islam considers it a sacred mission of religious honor to recapture Old Jerusalem and the El-Aqsa and Dome of the Rock mosques, which are located at the third-holiest site of their faith.

Map 2: King of the North

The Soviet Union Launches an All-Out Invasion. (Daniel 11:40-45)

Phases:

1 & 2: Soviets and their allies launch massive invasion from land, sea, and air.

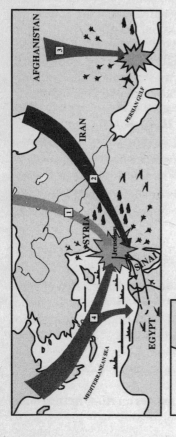

Map 2

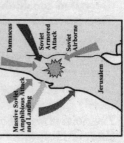

3: Soviets launch lightning attack on Strait of Hormuz from Afghanistan to close off oil from Persian Gulf.

4: Soviet navy makes large amphibious invasion. Hits hard and lands at Haifa, gateway to the Valley of Armageddon. Also lands on shores of Egypt.

Soviet commander moves rapidly through Israel on his way to Egypt and prepares to take Africa. (See Daniel 11:42-44.)

News from north and east troubles the Soviet leader: The Chinese and ten-nation-led Western forces are mobilizing in preparation for counterattack. Soviet commander regroups and moves back to Jerusalem. Then he is destroyed by divine intervention.

Map 3: Armies of the East and West

China and Ten Nations of Europe Counterattack. (Revelation 16:12, Daniel 11:44)

The Western nations led by the Antichrist and the oriental nations led by China attack the northern alliance of the Soviet Union. By both human and supernatural means, the Soviets are totally destroyed.

"I will drive the northern army [Soviets and their allies] far from you, pushing it into a parched and barren land, with its front columns going into the eastern sea and those in the rear into the western sea. And its stench will go up; its smell will rise" (Joel 2:20 NIV).

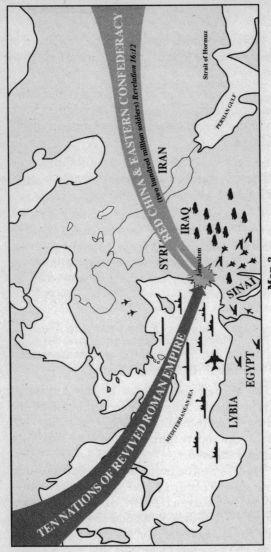

TEN NATIONS OF REVIVED ROMAN EMPIRE

SYRIA RED CHINA & EASTERN CONFEDERACY
(two hundred million soldiers) *Revelation 16:12*

Jerusalem

MEDITERRANEAN SEA

LYBIA

EGYPT

SINAI

IRAQ

IRAN

PERSIAN GULF

Strait of Hormuz

Map 3

"Son of man, prophesy against Gog [Soviet leader] and say: 'This is what the Sovereign Lord says: I am against you, O Gog, prince of Rosh, Meshech and Tubal. I will turn you around and drag you along. I will bring you from the far [extreme] north and send you against the mountains of Israel. Then I will strike your bow from your left hand and make your arrows drop from your right hand. On the mountains of Israel you will fall, you and all your troops and the nations with you. I will give you as food to all kinds of carrion birds and to the wild animals. You will fall in the open field, for I have spoken, declares the Sovereign Lord. I will send fire on Magog [the land of Russia] and on those who live in safety in the coastlands [the continents of the Gentile civilizations], and they will know that I am the Lord'" (Ezekiel 39:1-6 NIV).

Map 4: The Messiah Comes

Blood Shall Stand to the Horses' Bridles. (Revelation 14:19-20)

One of the most-often-quoted and least-understood prophecies concerning the last days is Revelation 14:19,20, which says: "And the angel swung his sickle to the earth, and gathered the clusters from the vine of the earth, and threw them into the great wine press of the wrath of God. And the wine press was trodden outside the city [Jerusalem]; and blood came out from the wine press, up to the horses' bridles, for a distance of two hundred miles."

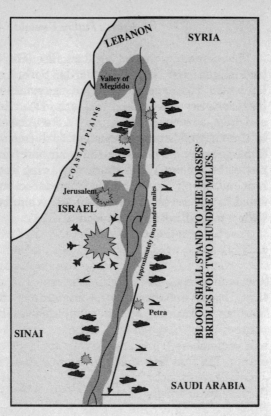

Map 4: Fault Line. The instant that the Messiah returns to the Mount of Olives, at the very place from which He ascended long ago, an earthquake will split the mountain, forming a new canal that will make Jerusalem a major inland seaport. The fault line will extend from just north of the Temple area in Jerusalem west to the Mediterranean at the site of ancient Azal and south to the Dead Sea (Zechariah 14:2-5).

This geological shift will cause the Dead Sea to overflow southward into the Wadi al-Arabah, which is a rift valley and a natural waterway. (See Ezekiel 47:1-11; Joel 3:16-18; and Isaiah 43:19.)

The map shows the only continuous valley of that length in Israel. It is the Jordan River Valley, which extends southward from the southern end of the Sea of Galilee through the Dead Sea and dried-up river bed called the Wadi al-Arabah, to the Gulf of Eilat (or Aqabah). The fiercest fighting will take place around Jerusalem and along the Jordan Valley. Man will bring such horrible carnage upon himself that blood will stand to the horses' bridles along this Jordan Valley, most of which is below sea level.

Israel's Miraculous Deliverance

In one of the most incredible miracles of all time, Israel will be converted to faith in her true Messiah and then miraculously protected. The prophet Zechariah, whose name means "Jehovah remembers," promises an amazing deliverance: "In that day I will make the clans of Judah like a firepot among pieces of wood and a flaming torch among sheaves, so they will consume on the right hand and on the left all the surrounding peoples, while the inhabitants of Jerusalem again dwell on their own sites in Jerusalem. The Lord also will save the tents of Judah first in order that the glory of the house of David and the glory of the inhabitants of Jerusalem may not be magnified above Judah.

"In that day the Lord will defend the inhabitants of Jerusalem, and the one who is feeble among them in that day will be like David, and the house of David will be like God, like the angel of the Lord before them. And it will come about in that day that I will set about to destroy all the nations that come against Jerusalem" (Zechariah 12:8,9).

As promised, God will strengthen the Israelis to fight with a ferocity never seen before on this earth. He will also supernaturally protect them from being annihilated. The reason for all of this is given in the next verse: "And I will pour out on the house of David and on the inhabitants of Jerusalem, the Spirit of grace and of supplication, so that they will look on Me [the Messiah, the Lord Jesus] whom they [Israel] have pierced; and they will mourn for him [the Messiah], as one mourns for an only son, and they will weep bitterly over Him, like the bitter weeping over a first-born" (Zechariah 12:10).

In this verse God Himself predicted that there would be a time when Israel would physically pierce Him. As we look through history, there is only one occasion on which this could have happened. It was when Israel nailed Jesus of Nazareth to the cross at Golgotha. This prophecy looks forward to that fateful moment when the sons of Israel will finally acknowledge that the One they pierced was none other than the God of Abraham, Jesus the Messiah.

Signs of Armageddon's Approach

All the conditions that the prophets have predicted would occur just before Armageddon are coming together before our eyes. In addition to the specific signs mentioned earlier, the general signs that Jesus predicted would precede His coming like "birth pangs" are increasing in frequency and severity:

Religious deceptions.

International revolutions.

Wars and rumors of wars.

Earthquakes.

Famines caused by population explosion and weather changes.

Plagues.

Global weather changes with resulting killer storms.

Increasing lawlessness and crime.

All the predicted signs are before us. No other generation has ever witnessed the simultaneous coming together of these prophetic events. It is because of this that I believe we are the generation that will see the Lord Jesus' return.

Time to Look Up

World events viewed through the grid of Bible prophecy indicate that we are rapidly moving toward the end of history as we know it.

The good news is this: Jesus Christ has promised that He will miraculously deliver all who believe in Him from this terrible holocaust. This miraculous deliverance, called the Rapture, is the event in which the Lord Jesus will mysteriously snatch every living true Christian out of the world in a split second. As we are secretly caught up in the clouds to meet the Lord, we will be miraculously transformed from mortal to immortal. Those who are part of this event will never know physical death (1 Corinthians 15:51-53 and 1 Thessalonians 4:15-18).

Then we will be taken to God the Father's house to be given rewards for every act of faith we have performed in this life (John 14:1-3). At the end of the Tribulation period, we will return to the earth with Jesus Christ, as His bride. And then, as kings and priests, we will help Him rule the new earth (Revelation 19:7-9; 20:6).

I pray that everyone who reads this booklet will be with us on that great day when the Lord Himself descends from heaven with a shout and catches up all living believers to meet Him in the air.